In My Mind's Eye

by

David James

Eloquent Books
New York, New York

Eloquent Books
An imprint of AEG Publishing Group
845 Third Avenue, 6th Floor - 6016
New York, NY 10022
www.eloquentbooks.com

ISBN: 978-1-60860-719-8

Printed in the United States of America

Book Design: SP

TABLE OF CONTENTS

1. Brussels and the Taxman. 5
2. The Bank Manager. 6
3. The Human "Race" 7
4. Colin McCrae, a tribute.. 9
5. Winters Hold. 11
6. A Xmas Tale. 13
7. The Doctor....He Can't Get Ill? 14
8. New Meaning. 15
9. She Of Course... 16
10. A Time To Dance.. 17
11. Seasons. 18
12. The World Of Being A Parent. 19
13. Stand In Meassured Silence. 21
14. Your'e Gone. 22
15. In My Mind When I wake. 24
16. The Farmer. 25
17. The Tooth Fairy Visits 26
18. Santa. 27
19. Xmas Blues. 29
20. Somewhere I am Thinking. 30
21. The Spell That Cant Be Broken. 31
22. Let Me Share Your Shadow. 32
23. Homecoming 34
24. My Friend. 36
25. You...My Thoughts. 37
26. Don't Tell Me. 38
27. Here Alone. 40
28. Sit Awhile. 41
29. The Politicians Lament. 42
30. Couldnt You Just Wait Awhile. 43
31. A Mortal Guy. 44
32. Heaven Can Wait. 46
33. Gentle As A Whisper Told. 47
34. Easter Thoughts. 48

Brussels and the Taxman

I ought to be happy, God knows I try,
But it's hard when the tax man is being so sly,

I get a good wage; well that's what I feel
But it seems it's all there for the taxman to steal,

Pay up for for this bit and pay up for that
No wonder in Westminster they are so fat

All this would be funny if it weren't such a crime
That they take the pay, while we do the time.

At the end of the tunnel there isn't a light,
Soon we'll be taxed for sleeping at night!

We need some fresh people to run all this show,
It sure can't be Labour or Liberal you know,

Can Tories deliver what we really need?
Or should we consider a total new breed?

We just want some fairness and common sense,
Not a spin merchant who sits on the fence,

A Churchill is wanted your countries in need,
It's crammed full of liars all driven by greed,

Now we have Brussels to help with the fun,
They spend all my money and answer to none,

They make the decisions yet we didn't choose
Just one referendum, our vote they would lose,

So here's to the future and lets have a say,
On why all these suits can spend all our pay!

The Bank Manager

My Bank Mans a cheerful chappie,
He’s got my money it makes him happy,

His welcomes always warm and kind,
A nicer man you couldn’t find,

He’ll help you with your pension deals,
even help you find new wheels,

But if you ask him for some cash,
his smile is gone in just a flash,

"Take’s" a word you must not use!
It gives our man the monetary blues,

He gets all hot and sprouts a rash
When you mention wanting cash

But as he seethes, just look forlorn
And tell him that your overdrawn

He’ll rage and cuss and rant and rave,
Probably hate you to his grave,

So always quit while you’re ahead
And hide your cash under the bed!

The Human "Race"

I sit here in my office just staring into space,
and find myself just wandering what is the human "race"?

Why do we have no time to live and talk to passers by
why is it that we seldom laugh but find the time to cry?

The world is just a run around and slowly sucks us in,
The vortex that is daily life, it really is a sin,

All through life we miss the point of why we are around,
If we stood back and took the time, the answer could be found,

For all the money in the world, the house, the car, the style,
Could not replace the things in life that truly are worthwhile,

Just take the time to look around right beneath your feet,
The things that matter most in life are cheap and always sweet

You take for granted all the things your given at your birth
Your kids are quite a marvel yet we seldom see their worth,

The sky above, the sun so bright, should all be on a par,
With making money as we strive to buy the newest car,

The time we give to family is never quite enough,
There's always something wrong at work that makes it really tough

But through all this you must decide just what you really need,
Can happiness be reached with cash?, or is it really greed?

And is the meek and lowly man who has some time to spend
The one who gets the most from life?, That really would depend,

On if you find your happiness is having lots of money
Or whether life's true gifts to you are simply bread and honey

And as I sit here deep in thought at why we are so blind
The answer to my question seems impossible to find,

For now my day has disappeared the clock has ticked away,
Oh there we are, I'll think again... perhaps some other day.

Colin McCrae...a tribute...

Up at five and really so keen,
To see the bond of man and machine

3 hours to drive to get to the start
We all have a laugh and so full of heart

We know it is early, the weather is damp
But we need to see cars come off the ramp

Through fog and rain we push on with style
We know the main man is due in a while

Then comes a whistle, the marshal says time
A car is now coming through forests of pine

Its howl is so frightening, like a banshee on heat
There is no escape, as we shuffle our feet

And suddenly now it's why we are here
McRae over crest of course in top gear!

It's been worth the wait, the weather, the toil,
To see the brave Scot here on home soil

But now there is silence, and it's deafening too
Cos you and the wee man have bid us adieu.

So rest in peace Colin you and your lad
You gave us your best, John be proud of your dad.

The memories you left us are above all the rest
You shone like a star, just simply the best.

Colin you're a mate and that's what we all thought

It made you a hero and that just can't be bought.

Now you're in heaven with your boy and at rest
But you left us the true meaning of FLAT OVER CREST!

God Bless Colin and Johnny, Rest in Peace. Read out on Sky and BBC at the memorial of Colin and his boy, tragically killed in a helicopter crash.....

"Winters hold"

Of winters use I'm sure not,
And Winters Cold I like not,
Its Frozen fingers trace the land,
Destroying Autumns fading hand

In deepest depths of foxes lair
Winter's presence still felt there,
Nothings spared from winter's call,
When Autumn bows her head to fall

For Mother Nature has good reason
She who masters change of season,
Birds fly south who know her best
Escape the Freezing winters quest

For us its such a curse of cold,
It tries to take the young and old,

But in it's ruthlessness and stance

Winters glory still enchants

In shapes and patterns it excels,

Natures canvass kiss and tells

Of beauty that is without equal

This continued Autumn sequel

And when the winters coolest fest

Is taking all to keep abreast,

Let mother nature have her way

As winters hold... Is here to stay.

A Xmas tale...

Father Christmas it would seem was never ever late

But this fine year while we all slept it seems he tempted fate,

For waking up with such a start, the clock had just chimed 3

This Christmas would come late for some it could be you and me!

So Rudolph raced off in the night with Santa on his sleigh

But they both new that all was lost as night drew into day

A sorry tear from Santa's eyes dropped slowly from the sky

And with it hope for all the kids as Xmas day drew nigh

But just as all seemed lost that night and misery was certain

Santa's tear was spotted by an elf behind a curtain,

Before it landed on the ground the elves were on a mission

300 sleighs with jingle bells all fighting for position

So off they went out here and there, no-one was forgotten

Without the elves we're all quite sure this Christmas would be rotten

The presents were all out on time and Santa cried a tear

But this time it was tears of joy his friends had saved our year

Now don't despair for Santa's plight and please sleep like a charm,

Cos Mrs. Clause has been to town for Santa's new alarm!

The Dr. He can’t get ill??

Now when your sick and quite unwell
There is someone you can tell

Our doctors they know every trick
By helping out when you are sick,

They have all types of colored pills
To cure all sorts of crazy ills

From spotty cheeks to fevered brow,
They sort you out I don't know how!,

They seem to have the Midas touch
Leg is broken.. here's a crutch!

All the answers are all there
When you’re in the Doctors chair

He'll probe you this way, poke you that
While giving you some friendly chat,

A doc must find the way ahead
When you are lying ill in bed,

But when the Doc gets very ill,
Who administers his pill?

Could it be the Docs immune,
to all the ills that we assume?

Or is he just a normal guy,
with aches and pains like you and I??

And gets a cough or nasty chill...

who says the Doctor can’t get ill??

New meaning.

My life has a new meaning
When you are at my side,

You give me back the feeling
Of love I cannot hide,

The sun just shines much brighter
Your presence makes it so

My step is that much lighter
Than you can ever know..

I could dance on rainbows
And make the rivers stand

If you were mine for always
And I could hold your hand

Through all life has to offer
So fine or very tough,

Your love would hold the answer
I could never get enough.

So stay with me forever
Hold me tight and never leave

for love has found a meaning
and a reason to believe.

She...of course.

The sun wakes up and casts an eye,
across the world I love,

Yet something seems quite different -
and its not from up above...

For time flies by, no question why
and days are just a blur

I try to blame the working game
...but really it is her,

The sparkle she puts in my day,
her smiles could light a palace,

They're given free, belong to me -
and given without malice,

So if you ask me what has changed? -
And why my life is heaven

it’s down to her, all I can be
and all the love she's given..

Time to dance

If love becomes your focus,
Then life will take your side,

As all at once your feelings
Now keep you warm inside,

When hearts that once were broken
Now beat with perfect rhyme,

Embrace the one who loves you
And mountains you can climb,

For love can mend a thousand ills
and soothe away your pain

Like strolling out with Angels
Like walking in the rain,

The warmth of Bluest Ocean
Will stem the tide of hurt

Loves own aura soothes the way
Never false or curt

So question not your heart again
When Love has shown its face

Don't let your head be master
Let hearts be judge of pace

Embrace what you are feeling
With all your might and stance

Let love come in and fill your life
There's always "time to Dance".

Seasons...

I've had my selfish reasons,
To keep love from my side,

the bitter twist like seasons,
The times that I have cried,

To take the hearts of others,
Just seems a thankless task,

With all loves complications,
With all that love will ask,

Throughout the times that bind me
And all that's gone before,

I found that love was empty
A challenge, ... nothing more,

We know there are four seasons
On which we all depend,

To bring the Sun the Rain the Snow
And year unto its end...

Unlike a star that shines a light,
Upon our darkest hour

I found true love a hurtful mate ,
And reckless in its power,

So what say I of poets tales
and loving without reasons ?

You keep love I'll hold you tight
to guide you through the seasons

The World of being a parent...

Without reason or rhyme we take on the task
Of bringing up youngsters, no questions we ask,

But what if we did, would results be the same?
Would we rush to the bedroom with only one aim?

Would our ardor be crushed by the thought of no sleep?
Knowing of just what hours you'll keep,

The wailing on high and nappies galore
Is only a taster of what is in store,

And don't think a day out will give you a break
Not with the clutter you'll now have to take!

With wipes and the nappies, a pushchair to load
The cars on the floor barely missing the road

Then off you all go, but soon you'll be met
With the Fimbles CD and "are we there yet?"

When you arrive they all want a wee,
Which isn't so easy now you have three?

So Dad heads for one loo while Mum to another
To relieve the toddlers, sisters and brother,

Then prams get filled and we are off at a gallop,
"Just watch where your going!", oh no, too late, Wallop!

So screams fill the air as they show you the grazes
Just how you keep going it really amazes,

Round for the groceries and shops as you pant,
"I want an ice cream" "oh no you can't!"

Then off for dinner but your not surprised
When hoops of spaghetti fly past your eyes,

Then comes the pudding, oh what a mistake!
2 wanted ice cream but you've got "em cake

Now dinner is over, the battle is won,
How did you cope before all this fun?

And when day is through and you've packed all away
And you've sung all the rhymes as in bed they lay,

You sit down and cuddle the one that you love
Open some wine and then thank God above

For all the tough work is sure not in vain,
And given the chance you'd do it again!!

Stand in measured silence...

If I could stand in silence,
for just a little time

And bask in wondered splendor of all that is divine

It seems to me, that all I see
and all I could achieve,

Stems from love and God above,
and reasons to believe,

But life can be so hard you see
and test our own resolve

To take a stand, walk hand in hand
with problems you must solve,

So in that whispered silence,
you must wait and watch a while,

Look all around at love unbound
and raise a knowing smile,

For we all have a place in time,
that's ours to use as such

In truth its only measured,
by the souls that we touch,

Though we may put great value
on the items that we own

The truest worth of what is first,
is love, our friends, our home.

Your gone...

I'm drowning in the silence
That's here now you are gone,
Can't see no rhyme or reason,
Cant hear or sing the song,

If love could talk and be so wise
so strange as though it seems
It's bound to say you own my heart
The answer to my dreams

But losing you has crushed me,
and love has passed me by
Is love so wise to cause my tears
And leave me hear to cry??

No Golden Fleece could tempt me
or life that never dies
Nor paradise where angels sing
Replace you in my eyes.

And though I may be lost for good

in hurt that seems immense

I hold on to the thoughts of you

the pain is less intense

In my Mind...when I awake...

Your there in my mind when I wake...

Your there with the breath that I take,

You walk in my dreams when I sleep,

Your soul is the one that I keep..

When I met you my world opened wide

Cant imagine you not by my side...

Should your life become weary and tough

And your heart is just crying enough...

I will be there as long as you need,

And together we both will succeed...

So take heart there's someone out there

Who loves you.......and always will care...

The Farmer

What makes the farmer happy? is a question I should ask,
It takes more than a sandwich and a drink out of his flask,

It takes more than an auction where his beasts take all the praise
It takes more than a crop of spuds that he will surely raise,

It takes more than a field of hay just basking in the sun,
It takes more than the lively calf just kicking out in fun,

It takes more than a silage pit that's bursting to the seams
It takes more than a bank account that's always in the teens,

It takes more than a pretty wife who cooks a meal or two
It takes more than a faithful dog who wouldn't work for you

It takes more than a combine that has worked without a fault,
It takes more than a plough that never breaks a single bolt,

There is a way to get our man just jumping up with glee
To make his day and have a laugh along with you and me,

To get our friend the farmer man to flex his chuckle muscles
Tell him he's just had a cheque from those nice men in Brussels.

The tooth fairy visits..??

The tooth fairy came but we never met,
Though gone are my teeth that she came to get,

A visit she paid to gather my teeth,
I lifted my pillow and peered underneath

And to my delight my teeth they had gone
Replaced by a coin so brightly it shone

So up with a start I leaped out of bed
To catch me a fairy but met Mum instead..

"What's all this racket?" she said in a thrice
"Look Mum a coin", "yes Dear, That's nice!"

So trust what you're told "cos this is all true
and lo and behold it could happen to you!!

Santa...

Now out across the big divide
twixt land and frozen sea
there lives a man with heart of gold
who's known to you and me.

He loves all children we are sure
He never lets them down
He knows if you've been good or bad
In village or in Town

His name is Santa Claus you see
And he is oh so wise
With trusty friends the reindeer
He soars across the skies

And through the night on Christmas eve
While all good kiddies snooze
He makes his way around the world
He has no time to lose

Rudolph with his shiny nose
Is lighting Santa's way
He weaves a magic spell of gifts
In time for Christmas day

And in the morning all awake
And clap their hands with glee
At all the gifts so neatly wrapped
Around the Christmas tree

So here's to Santa, Rudolph too
They really are the best
He's heading off twixt land and sea
till next year for a rest......

So thank old Santa Rudolph too
For making all your dreams come true
And if you've been as good as gold
He'll come next year....so I've been told....!

Xmas blues...?

The tinsels looking worse for wear
The Fridge is back to being bare

The Christmas tree is on a lean
Scattered needles need a clean

The house is like a battle zone
Cos everyone has been at home

There's paper here there's paper there
In every corner every chair !!

The turkeys just an empty shell
The mistletoe has kissed, wont tell

The heating bill is twice the size
The Postman's stuffed with Gran's mince pies

So all this madness we endure
Must mean its Xmas time for sure

But now its past and we can rest
As everyone has done their best

And as we sink into a chair
Our eyes just fixed, an empty stare

We sit and wonder was it worth
The drunken nights the extra girth

But when December comes around
A second wind we will have found

So here's to next years Christmas time
And worry not about this rhyme... !

Somewhere I am thinking...

If you've woken from your slumber
rubbed the sleep out of your eyes
take a glance so high above you
Deep into the bluest skies

As somewhere out there on this planet
Someone's thinking just of you
Though distance seems to pull you under
Love can cross that sky so blue

So glance above the highest mountain
Look beyond the distant haze
Far beyond the seas horizon
Someone's counting down the days

When we can meet and kiss so tender
hold each other really tight
Beneath the sky we shared together
dreaming each and every night.

The spell that can’t be broke...

Sitting here without you casts a spell that cant be broke
The empty room the silent air so thick that I could choke,
You owned the deepest part of me our love so much entwined
With so much ease you lead the way I followed on behind
I walked upon your shadow soft and light as I could dare
With growing fear that I may look and you would not be there
But while I lay beside you, watching beauty as it slept
I knew I couldn’t read your mind, the secrets that it kept
You Heart belonged to someone else and I was last to know
I told myself that you were mine and you would never go
So though I may have lost the love that made me so complete
I’ll wait until the end of time or my heart stops to beat.

Let me share your shadow.

If I could share your shadow
For just the briefest time

And sink into your open arms
your body next to mine

This planet could stop turning
The sun could fade and die

I could take all this and more
No need to ask me why

If I could share your shadow
For just the briefest time

Words could lose their meaning
Poems lose their rhyme

The sky could fall tomorrow
The rivers lose their way

With you here right beside me
Who needs another day?.

If I could share your shadow
The song could lose its tune

Seasons could forget to change
Or come around too soon

So hold me closer to you
So close I hear you breathe

Let me share your shadow
And promise not to leave.

Homecoming...

The sea breeze stings this weary face
As home comes into view

My journeys end is drawing near
Cant help but think of you

Though I am almost broken
You stand out like a star

That guides me ever onwards
From foreign lands afar

I kept you here beside me
Through all the the hurt and pain

Just dreaming of the the day I'm home
To share our love again

I step upon this hallowed land
The place that I call home

Your there to take me by the hand
We've both been so alone

And as I gaze into your eyes
I feel the hurt and pain

That you had felt while I was gone
I new I was to blame

But as we reach the harbor
My head bows to the ground

Its all a dream and I recall
The new love you have found

And though my heart is broken
And life for me stands still

I carried all the dreams with me
That you could love me still

I kept you here beside me
though you would never know

That I was thinking of you,
that love in time may grow.

...My Friend.

They say that beauties just skin deep
that someone's "soul" is yours to keep,

that night will follow on from day,
and real love won't fade away,

That Childs innocence is pure
and broken hearts still have no cure

that oceans secrets stay untold.
And one true love is hard to hold.

They say that you must follow rules
That love is company for fools

But I believe that life is yours
And opens such amazing doors

If you embrace it with both hands
And worry not where your fate lands

For fools may not have high regard
They seldom play the winning card

But me I'd rather simple be
Than lose my friend, that's you, you see...

You...My Thoughts

To think that you are sound asleep
and night is by your side

is all I think of thru the day
the feelings I just hide...

Until you wake and call again
or send a simple line ...

My heart will beat a slower tune
and nothing seems to rhyme...

The air is never quite as sweet
the pace of life a blur

when work is all I have to do
but all I want is her...

So as you wake and rub your eyes
the sun so bright above,

Just send a line that you are mine
my one true perfect love...

... Don’t tell me...

Don’t tell me that life is tough
Don’t tell me you’ve had enough

Don’t tell me your feeling sad
Don’t tell me it makes you mad

Don’t tell me that nothings right
Don’t tell me about your plight

Don’t tell me its so unfair
Don’t tell me that I don’t care

Don’t tell me about your woes
Just take a hint from one who knows

That we all moan and curse our fate
When we are but a minute late

And shops aren’t open through the night
The weathers wet or suns too bright

That money never stretches far
Or you cant have a nice new car

That eating out you had to wait
There’s not enough upon your plate.

For I am he who sees the child
with furrowed brow, so meek and mild

That hasn’t food enough to eat
Or shoes upon their blistered feet

That takes a beating every day
that wishes Dad would go away

The child that weeps and no-one hears
And being brave beyond their years

That hasn't Mum or Daddy there
That hasn't anyone to care

That shivers in the darkest night
Yet starves beneath the sun so bright

So don't tell me about your day
How everyone got in your way

Or someone hasn't done their best
Or all you want is home and rest

For in this world we call our home
So many children cope alone

They've not a care about such things
Or any gift that money brings

They only have what God allows
And he alone doth mop their brows

So think before you next complain
And don't tell me about your "pain" ..

Here Alone …

I’m here alone, just thinking of tomorrow
When once again you’ll be here by my side

I cant find the words I should be saying,
The feelings deep within, I cannot hide,

You make the heavens look like they are borrowed,
The stars, like they are worthless specs of light,

Your beauty takes the breath of guardian angels,
That comforts us in deepest darkest night,

your touch means I could jump the highest mountain
Your beauty like a castle in the sky

I could take all heartache life has waiting,
You'd never feel the need to ask me why..

When life has run its course and I am wilting
My Soul it comes to rest on hallowed ground

I'll thank the angels for their love and patience
in bringing me the love that I have found.

Though I am all alone here in the darkness
my life just fading gently with the light

I have the thoughts of you to carry with me
the deepest darkest corners still seem bright.

Sit Awhile…

Sometimes I chance to sit awhile
And take a breath of life
As day to day we miss the point
And moan about the strife

We miss the times that matter most
We're blinded by our need
To grab the things that money brings
I guess we call it greed.

But now its calm the world is still
I pause and then reflect
what life should mean in all its forms
perhaps just more respect.

For friends I've met along the way
have made it all worthwhile
they've held me tight when it seemed right
and gone the extra mile.

I know you've given me so much
I thank you from my heart
and though the distance may be great
we're never far apart..x

The Politicians Lament.

I cannot be all that you see
its quite impossible for me

I cannot live a life of lies
For all and sundry to despise

I cannot speak of facts unknown
I care not if I am alone

I Never seek another’s trust
I think that honesty's a must

I speak when only spoken to
I seldom ask what I can do

I ask much less of those I meet
No promises I dare to keep

So why should I just listen in
To an MP with cheesy grin

When without feeling without love
He ignores the words above

And tells me what I need to hear
as soon as polling day is near

So I will stay an honest chap
and take no notice of his crap.

Couldn’t you just wait…

Couldn’t you just wait a while
Couldn’t you just let me smile

Let me have just one more day
Holding you in my own way

Couldn’t you just play along
Like singing to a favourite song

Knowing what you meant to me
Or were we never meant to be...

I gave you all I had to give
And all i wanted was to live

Inside your memories and heart
never thinking we would part

So let me play another song
Hold you ‘cos it can't be wrong

Couldn’t you just be with me
Was I the only one to see

That love can be a poisoned pill
Once taken you are always ill

So I may be the one to blame
With all to lose and most to gain

But loving you means no regret
You'll be the one I won’t forget.

A Mortal Guy.

What chance have I?
A mortal Guy
Of saving life and limb

When all around
All that is found
Is avarice and sin.

Our leaders gave their very soul
To bankers and their money

Then spent it all on second homes
And I don’t think it's funny

I sit amongst a ruined state
That once stood like a beacon

seldom ever second rate
And never ever beaten

But in our country all is lost
No hope and much less Glory

That’s all we have to give our kids
It's such a woeful story.

So what of I the Mortal Guy
Who sits alone in wonder

at pure contempt at those who lead
and surely pull us under.

So hear a warning when it sounds
I have no axe to grind

But cheats and liars all around
are all that you will find

No sense of duty one and all
They whimper so when rumbled

With hand inside the public purse
As country slowly crumbled

No Englishman can have a say
Must only think of others

No mention of equality
This happy band of brothers.

So i must seek another land
That welcomes harder workers

The UK now walks hand in hand
with liars thieves and shirkers...

Where once there stood a country true
A Shining ray so bright

Now just a shell of all we knew
So please turn off the lights..

Heaven Can Wait

The day has wandered into night
and slowly fades and dies

I lie with you and hold you tight
And look into your eyes

Your look it melts me to the core
No rival heaven knows

You never leave me wanting more
More perfect than the Rose

If i should die before the dawn
And hear an angels voice

My last wish before i'm gone
would be a simple choice

For you to warm my very heart
And take the pain of leaving.

That we should never be apart
Or share the pain of grieving

So lay your head so softly here
And sleep until it’s late

I'll never see you shed a tear
So heaven it can wait … x

Gentle As a Whisper Told

Gentle as a whisper told
Soft as new born babe to hold

As quiet as the hush of prayer
As gentle as a breath of air

As strong as tallest forest pine
As safe the hands of father time

As proud as any lion born
As sure the Rose with prickly thorn

As fine a gift that God could bring
As fresh the flowing mountain spring

Your heart was pure as driven snow
It's thoughts alone for me to know

So having you to hold and love
Was like a blessing from above,

I will live my life content
Knowing you were heaven sent.

Dedicated To Tracey and late husband Alan.

Easter Thoughts

At Easter time its understood
That evil couldn't triumph good

For all the sins that man has done
were taken on by only one

Though he was special its agreed
He gave himself for mankind’s need

No selfish thought to save his skin
A saviour true was ushered in

Though man behaved with such contempt
Of feelings he was not exempt

The saviour knew that there was light
And man could put his wrongs to right

So all in all the lessons learnt
That even with your bridge's burnt

It needs just one with faith in you
To make things work and see it through

So even if your faith is shallow
You can walk the straight and narrow

There is always someone there
Just ask him with a simple prayer.

Lightning Source UK Ltd.
Milton Keynes UK
28 October 2009

145503UK00001B/37/P

9 781608 607198